OPEN AIR DESIGNS

OPEN AIR DESIGNS

Evaluating, Planning, and Building the Perfect Outdoor Living Space

by John Driemen

HPBooks

A FRIEDMAN GROUP BOOK

Copyright © 1988 by Michael Friedman Publishing Group, Inc.

Published by HPBooks
a division of
Price Stern Sloan, Inc.
360 North La Cienega Boulevard
Los Angeles, California 90048

Library of Congress Cataloging-in-Publication Data

Driemen, John.
  Open air designs : evaluating, planning, and building the perfect outdoor
living space / by John Driemen.
        p.   cm.
  Includes index.
  ISBN 0-89586-718-4 : $24.95. ISBN 0-89586-717-6 (pbk.) : $9.95
    1. Decks (Architecture, Domestic).   2. Patios.   3. Landscape
architecture. I. Title.
TH4970.D75 1988
643'.55—dc19   87-23068
                                                                                  CIP

OPEN AIR DESIGNS: Evaluating, Planning, and Building the Perfect Outdoor
Living Space
was prepared and produced by
Michael Friedman Publishing Group, Inc.
15 West 26th Street
New York, New York 10010

Editor: Tim Frew
Art Director: Mary Moriarty
Designer: Devorah Levinrad
Photo Editor: Christopher Bain
Production Manager: Karen L. Greenberg

Typeset by B.P.E. Graphics
Color separations by South Sea International Press Ltd.
Printed and bound in Hong Kong by Leefung-Asco Printers Ltd.

Acknowledgments

I'd like to thank my friend and colleague Lloyd Jafvert for checking some of the technical points in this book, for timely redirection when I took a wrong turn, and for putting up with a lot of the nonsense that seems to be attendant to any book project. I would also like to thank my former associates at *Decorating Remodeling Magazine* and particularly Karen Saks. They showed me the wisdom of sticking to my guns when it came to speaking up for the kind of practical information contained in this book.

John Driemen

CONTENTS

Introduction

I n the 1940s, people began fleeing the city for the suburbs; there, they discovered the great outdoors which lay in their own backyards. Today, the barbecue and the ritual mowing of lawns have become a form of suburban Zen. More recently—due in part to a wider array of readily available remodeling products and strong homeowner desire to get directly involved in home improvement—the backyard has become the raw material from which to develop an outdoor living environment. Only kitchen and bathroom remodeling is more popular than backyard deck and patio projects. Few would argue that the enjoyment that comes from using a deck or patio far outweighs the cost of building a pleasant outdoor environment.

Magazines have been quick to recognize the trend toward more elaborate outdoor designs, and devote ample space to presenting lavishly styled yards that few can afford. Too often what's missing from the magazines is the attempt to point out the principles that form the foundation of any good design. Once explained, these principles can help homeowners plan and build practical, yet beautiful decks and patios.

Nancy Hill

My intent with this book is to link pictures of beautiful outdoor spaces to the realities of your own backyard. Much of the information you find here is immediately useful. If you're handy with tools, this information will be a good primer to get you started on a deck or patio project. If you prefer to leave the dirty work to others, you'll find suggestions to help you deal intelligently with design and building professionals. There is a step-by-step presentation of what you need to know to design your outdoor space, as well as a materials section that shows what to use, how to use it, and why. Too often, for the sake of beauty, people shelve their common sense and create something that is dangerous. Included here are pictures that clearly show what not to do when designing your deck or patio. It is my hope that after reading this book you will be able to design, plan, and if you choose, build the perfect outdoor space for your needs.

Vern Green

CHAPTER 1

An Extension of Your Lifestyle

From clothes to cars, eating to entertaining, the emphasis today is on things that are casual and informal. Nowhere is this more noticeable than in how we use our backyard. Gone are the days when the yard was just so much grass with flower borders here and there, a small plot for growing vegetables, and a few square yards of bricks next to the back door where the barbecue sat. Today, many people count their yard almost as another room, a versatile open-air family center, perfect for cooking, eating, entertaining, or just relaxing.

But an outdoor space doesn't grow automatically from the fertile soil that's been home to dandelions and crabgrass. Like any other room addition, it must be planned, built, and paid for before it can be enjoyed. The purpose of this book is to guide you through the steps that transform a yard into an outdoor family room.

We live in an era when everyone wants everything in a hurry. If you are suddenly hungry, there are hundreds of fast-food restaurants to provide exactly what you want, right now. Unfortunately, this attitude sometimes extends to home improvement, as well, especially outdoor projects such as decks and patios. And, too often, such projects are sloppily planned and shoddily built in an effort to enjoy the new deck or patio as soon as possible.

Courtesy American Wood Council

Robert Perron

Facing Page: On this elevated deck, additional seating is built into the 36-inch-high safety rail. The moveable table is built from the same material used for the deck.

Above: Shaded areas are easily created with an overhead trellis system. Here, sections of pre-made lattice are installed on top of a roof structured from 2x8s. Lattice is sold in 2x8 and 4x8 panels and can be easily cut to any size. Pre-routered border and trim pieces make it easy to join panel sections and create a finished look around the edges.

The products currently popular today are pre-cut deck kits in sizes and shapes that are adaptable to most backyard situations. For a more custom-looking deck, some lumberyards and home centers offer computer-design services. The prevalent assumption among retailers is that one of these approaches must be right for you. Many people, regrettably, fall for this, and they buy and build a deck only to be disappointed later when they realize that their backyard improvement does not fit the style of the house, or that it cuts down rather than increases the usability of their yard and doesn't provide the anticipated room for enjoyment. It's not even a question of money because, surprisingly, a small deck—if you build it yourself—can cost less than $700. But once it's there, an unsuitable deck becomes a monument to haste and a less than satisfactory addition that must be lived with.

For these reasons, you should approach any outdoor project carefully and be aware that what you do will not only affect your lifestyle, but will also have a major impact on the value of your property.

A common mistake many people make is to consider outdoor improvements separately from the existing house. This is wrong because your house establishes the physical and psychological boundaries of your lifestyle. If you've chosen a traditional or Colonial house, it's probably because you like the comfort and prac-

This small, low-cost deck includes built-in seating, which also functions as a safety railing. Though railings are not usually required by code on decks less than 30 inches above grade, they are a good precautionary measure, especially if you have small children or if the deck will be used by elderly people.

Peter Paige

Materials often thought to be intended solely for commercial use can be excellent choices for a high-tech look. Here, concrete planters provide an enclosure for a roof-top swimming pool, while a changing cabana finished in stucco hides the building's mechanical system.

ticality inherent in these designs. But it also establishes what you don't like—such things, perhaps, as the gingerbread ornamentation of the Victorian style or the functional clean lines of the contemporary style. Whatever your taste, it's important that your outdoor space exists in harmony with what you already have and that you feel as comfortable stepping out as you do stepping in.

A more subjective and less noticeable aspect of the same question is that outdoor space is architecture. To work well, an open-air design must be planned with the same care and attention to detail as the best kitchen. It must have the flexibility to meet most of your current family needs and, within limits, be adaptable to meet unforeseen changes in lifestyle later on. For this to happen you must develop a specific design program in the same way you would for a family-room addition or a bathroom remodeling. Unless you clarify your objectives and put your ideas on paper, your deck might not fulfill all your needs. For example, a deck planned for the needs of a young family might not work as a place for a large outdoor party.

Another consideration, which many people forget about or dismiss as unimportant, is insects. Being outdoors is not very pleasant in many parts of the country. If you live in an area that has an insect problem, you should consider a design that provides a

Jerry Howard/Positive Images

Problems inherent to mortar-laid patio installations are seen here. Many of the mortar joints are cracked, most likely the result of frost heaves. Excess mortar along the joints indicates that cracks have been previously repaired. For information on how to avoid this problem turn to page 76.

screened sanctuary so that you can use your outdoor space even in times of bad infestations. A point to remember when planning a screened area is to always install screening material under the floor or deck boards. The best window screening available won't protect you if you leave the floor vulnerable.

Outdoor Space Options
Decks

Decks are the most popular outdoor room additions for several reasons. They can be built so the deck floor is level with the floor of the adjoining room, thus combining the two into a single indoor/outdoor space. When located directly off a kitchen or dining room, the deck provides an area for outdoor entertaining, a place for the barbecue, or an *alfresco* dining area. Decks can be any size, because they are engineered structures, like

The L-shape bench, made from 2x2 stock with a 2x4 trim border, is an important design element on this deck. However, because there is a long drop to the yard below, the bench should have been built with a back to function as a safety rail.

houses, and because they are above the grade level, water drains naturally from them.

Gazebos

If you have the yard space and envision your outdoor room as a retreat from household activities, you might consider building a gazebo. Gazebos originated in Victorian England as freestanding buildings within a formal garden. Their purpose was to provide a place to rest that also offered a tantalizing view of the surrounding scenery. Though many people still think of gazebos as elegant little eight-sided structures with ornate latticework, today the term is used loosely to describe any freestanding backyard structure that provides a sheltered place outdoors.

Considering the evolution of basic American housing styles, the gazebo actually performs the same function as the screened porch of forty years ago—a feature that has all but

Below: The lace-like quality long associated with gazebo design is enhanced here through the use of vinyl-coated wire—similar to the material used in closet storage systems—as the principal building material.

Above: Isolated from the rest of the yard, this traditional-looking gazebo fulfills it's function as an out-of-the-way retreat.

Courtesy of Georgia-Pacific Corporation

Sandra Dos Passos

Margaret Hensel/Positive Images

Many people feel that using stone paving materials laid on-grade creates a desirable natural setting—an area that is more an "environment" and less a "structure."

disappeared from most modern housing.

Because the gazebo is a freestanding structure, building one requires the same sort of planning that would go into a garage. There must be a foundation, and the framing must meet all applicable building codes.

Patios

When the centerpiece of your outdoor room is going to be on-grade, the simplest and least expensive option is to build a patio of brick, stone, or poured concrete and accessorize it with landscaping features, such as planting beds, berms, and retaining walls. Because patios are not structural, their shape and size is limited only by the imagination. And if your principal outdoor interest is gardening, a patio with interconnected paths can be the best way to provide a functional outdoor space that doesn't take anything away from the landscape.

Derek Fell

CHAPTER 2
Evaluating and Planning

Below: Always be sensitive to the possibilities of the site. This spa, part of a larger open-air design, is well integrated into the surrounding water; the overall effect is that of a pleasure barge that has temporarily docked.

Facing page: A trellis of 2x4s, supported by 4x4 posts and attached to the house using a box beam as a ledger, defines the space around this brick patio, giving it a room-like feel.

Robert Perron

Christopher Bain

Before you can build what you want, you have to know what you have. The very best open-air designs incorporate existing physical features, such as trees, into their final plan, which can mean a substantial savings. Surveying your yard to assess the pros and cons should be done with care and organization. Even if you plan to have the rest of the work contracted, this survey is something you should do yourself. A hands-on familiarity with your yard will be invaluable when it comes to working up a design that meets your needs.

The first task in assessing your yard is the easy one: Just spend a little time in it. Pick a sunny day so you can note the sun's position at various times. As the sun moves around, you will get an accurate picture of how the areas of sun and shade change as the day progresses.

This information will be

helpful when it comes time to plan activities and seating areas for your deck or patio. It will also give you an idea about what kind of planting—for sun or shade—you'll need for the different parts of your yard.

On the subject of the weather, try to ascertain the direction of the prevailing winds. If you have existing trees, do they function as a windbreak? If not, you might consider adding a row of fast-growing evergreens. And

there's a rainy-day chore, too: Discover if there are any areas where puddles form after heavy storms.

Continue your backyard tour by assessing the views. Many people routinely locate a deck or patio directly off the back door. But if you don't like what you see as you survey your yard from that position, consider another site that looks out onto more enjoyable scenery. The importance of views works in reverse, too. Go to the far corners of your

Christopher Bain

Wire construction not only creates a gazebo with soft interior lighting, but also makes an ideal growing trellis for climbing plants.

yard and look back toward the house. If you're not impressed, it's a good indication that some landscaping and planting are needed.

Next in your yard assessment, locate all of the existing physical features, such as trees, shrubs, and sheds, and mark their location on a rough plan—a sort of "as built" drawing for your yard. What you do here will become the basis for all new design work. While you're locating the physical features, you should

Because of its small size and ability to be laid in a variety of interlocking patterns, brick is an ideal material to use for walkways and patios. Brick patterns let you mix traditional and contemporary as in this example, where a loose basket weave pattern alternates with a running bond pattern.

Jerry Howard/Positive Images

also be establishing any grade changes. These, too, must be marked on the rough plan, because grade locations are important in planning for proper drainage. Grades are important for aesthetic reasons, too. The tops of fences and retaining walls should be at a constant height above grade, so as the grade changes, the various sections of fence or wall must be adjusted.

Before you take the field, stop in at the planning and zoning department at your lo-cal city hall. The odds are good that they will have a site plan of your house and yard on file. If so, ask them for a copy. A site plan is important because it establishes the legal boundaries of your property, which are important to know if your zoning department has setback requirements—that is, the required distance that any new construction must be set back from the lot line. If no site plan exists, the planning department may require you to have a survey and site plan

Decorative planter walls can provide the same function as a fence, defining boundaries and creating privacy. On a smaller scale, these walls can work as sculptural accessories or break up a large outdoor area into several smaller ''rooms.''

Nancy Hill

done, at your own expense, before they will issue a permit for any new construction.

Site plans may also show land contours and note tree positions. But because site plans exist mostly to establish the location of the house within the property, they may not accurately describe existing conditions.

To create an accurate existing-conditions plan, make sure you have the proper tools. For measuring, a fifty- or hundred-foot flexible tape measure works best. For determining grade, you'll need mason's string, some stakes you can pound into the ground, and a line level—a tiny level that attaches to the string. Finally, buy a T-square, a ruler, and plenty of eleven-by-fourteen-inch (or larger) graph paper. If you feel like treating yourself, buy an architect's scale. Finished landscape plans are customarily drawn using a one-eighth scale, that is, one inch equals eight feet, or one-eighth of an inch equals a foot. While you can use the eighth markings on a ruler to do this, the architect's scale makes the job much easier and is well worth the five dollars it costs. In scaling your drawing, remember that graph paper squares are one-quarter inch, so each square represents two feet. Soft lead pencils and an artist's eraser are other worthwhile purchases.

If you've measured for landscaping before, you might feel comfortable taking location measurements and determining grade changes at the same

time. For beginners it's best to separate these tasks and to locate the physical features first.

The first measurements to take are those of your house, or at least the outside wall that will adjoin the deck or patio. Start with an overall measurement and then take individual, running measurements to locate the positions of windows, doors, steps, chimneys, overhangs, or any other feature that might have a bearing on the eventual outdoor design. Window locations, for example, are extremely important to

An ashlar retaining wall—comprised of flat, hewn stones—adds a rustic touch to this otherwise masonry-dominated patio. Note how existing trees and shrubs create privacy along all but a short section of the yard's perimeter.

Michael Selig

Saxon Holt

Above: Randomly patterned flagstones bordered by a decorative railing and newel posts give this intimate outdoor area the feel of an old-time porch.

Facing page: Painting your deck is an option when you don't want the look of natural wood. Most paint manufacturers sell products for this purpose; you can choose between latex and alkyd based paints, although there will usually be a urethane additive to promote better wear and to provide protection against the elements.

good design, because they are the transition points between the indoor and outdoor spaces. A good outdoor design will create beautiful views from inside the house, too.

Let's say the distance across the back wall of the house is forty-five feet and four inches. Note this on your graph paper and then start over. This time measure from the end of the wall to the first window or door or whatever. In this example, we'll say that there's a picture window that starts nine feet in from the corner of the wall and that the window is six feet across. Mark both these distances on the graph paper. Continuing the running measurements, you find a three-foot-wide back door that's exactly ten feet from the end of the window. Mark down this information, too. By measuring these short increments across the whole wall, you can fix the exact locations of all doors, windows, and other features. When you have completed the running measurements, their totals should add up the overall distance you first measured.

Using the known positions you've established on the back wall of your house, you can begin to locate the trees and other landscaping. At this point, you'll have to dust the cobwebs off your memory and recall the principles of triangulation that you learned back in high school math—it's the trick that lets you determine the location of an unknown point by measuring from two known locations. Start with the trees, measuring to the first tree from two known points on the house. When you mark these measurements on the graph paper, it will establish the exact location of the tree. Now the tree becomes a known point to help locate the next feature. Measuring is a two-person activity: one to pull the end of the tape to the point being measured and call off the distance, the other to hold the tape reel and mark the dis-

Robert Perron

tances on the graph paper.

Information about the location of certain yard features may have to come from other sources. This is true for underground utilities, such as incoming water and sewer lines, gas lines, and electrical cables if you have underground service. Before starting any excavation, these utility lines must be located. Hitting one of them with a posthole auger or back hoe can result in expensive repairs and cause great delays. Information concerning the location of underground lines can be attained from the utility companies.

If you have a septic system rather than a city sewer, you must determine the location of the holding tank. This can be more difficult than finding a gas line, since companies that install septic tanks might not keep records. If you are not the first owner of the house, you will have to locate the drain lines and the tank yourself. A good clue is a stake or a small pipe in the backyard. This marks the access point to the tank, which can be opened for clean-out. After locating the tank, go into the house and look for the points where the three- or four-inch waste stacks exit through the sill plate. Generally, the horizontal waste lines leading to the tank run perpendicular to the house for ten or fifteen feet, then join at a Y-junction so that only a single line enters the tank. Septic waste lines are at least eighteen inches below the surface and may be as

Derek Fell

The versatility of brick as a building material is well illustrated here, where it surrounds the pool, stairways, a retaining wall, and an upper deck.

deep as the local frost line. Before serious excavation begins, you might have to do some careful exploratory digging to establish the exact locations.

Determining Grade Changes

Your eyes can tell you where even subtle grade changes occur. By doing a quick visual analysis of your yard, you can pick the points that should be measured accurately.

If your yard appears relatively flat, start by pounding a stake into the ground near the back door. Attach the mason's string to the stake, adjusting it to a height that corresponds to the inside floor level. Now run the string with the line level attached out to the end of the lot at what you think is the same level. Have the person holding the end of the string pull it tight and then attach the line level. Move the string up or down until the level bubble is centered. Move the line level and repeat the leveling procedure at several points along the string line. With the string level across the entire length of the yard, use a tape measure to note the distance from the ground to the string. Mark the distance in plus or minus inches. For example, if the floor height you've established at the back door is twenty-four inches above grade and your first measuring point along the string is thirty-one inches above grade, you know that

Sometimes the most effective way to integrate a deck with the landscape is to increase the grade height in the yard. This type of grading must be done with a small-tracked vehicle equipped with a front loader. In some situations, a back-hoe will also be needed.

Christopher Bain

Treated landscape timbers, similar to the old-fashioned, creosote railroad ties, joined together with 12-inch spikes make sturdy retaining walls. When built in a step pattern, they will follow grade changes. Timbers also work well for stairs—functioning as both tread and riser.

the grade has dropped by seven inches and you mark that point as minus seven inches.

It's not necessary to check your entire yard, but if you have a rough idea where you would like to position your deck, you should determine all grade changes along the perimeter. Likewise, if you're building a fence, you should establish the grade along the entire fence run.

Finally, there are a few easily observed conditions that have a bearing on what you might do. If you have children, pay attention to where they play. The reasons why children gravitate to a particular spot are less important than the fact that they do. If a play area is part of your plan, try to develop a design that locates it where your children are already comfortable. Otherwise, you may find that the play area you build goes unused.

Another thing to observe are the nonplanned pathways through your yard. A path is the shortest distance between two points for both adults and kids. The worn marks in the lawn are a pretty good indication of what the shortest distance is and where a real path should be located.

With all the existing features noted on a rough drawing of your yard, you can start designing your outdoor space. At this point don't worry if your drawing doesn't appear to be accurate. As long as the measurements are correct, a trained draftsman can turn your drawing into an accurate blueprint.

After making copies of your rough drawing, use tracing paper to try out different ideas and designs. Don't expect to get a "right one" on the first try. Even if you don't intend to do the final design work yourself, your tracing paper sketches can help organize your thinking and establish your priorities.

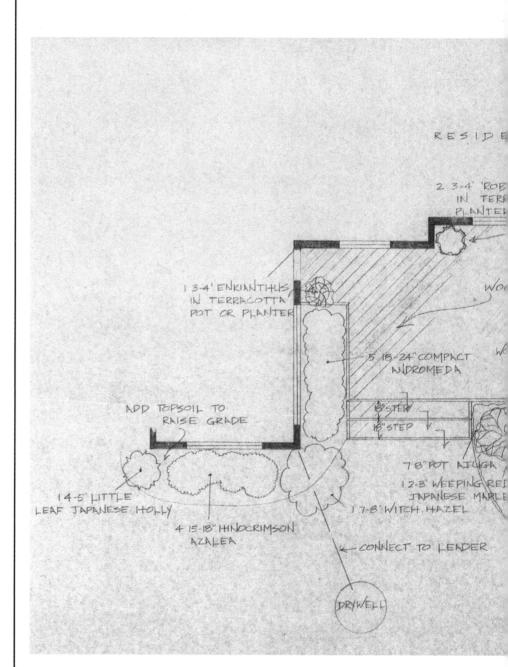

RESIDE

2 3-4' 'ROB
IN TER
PLANTE

1 3-4' ENKIANTHUS
IN TERRACOTTA
POT OR PLANTER

WOO

5 18-24" COMPACT
ANDROMEDA

W

ADD TOPSOIL TO
RAISE GRADE

8"STEP

16"STEP

7 8"POT AJUGA

1 2-3' WEEPING RED
JAPANESE MAPLE

1 4-5' LITTLE
LEAF JAPANESE HOLLY

1 7-8' WITCH HAZEL

4 15-18" HINOCRIMSON
AZALEA

CONNECT TO LEADER

DRYWELL

A typical plan for a deck addition shows the deck in relation to the house, the location of existing plantings, as well as new plantings to be implemented as part of the landscaping project. Scale is ¼ inch. In this plan even the direction of the deck boards is noted.

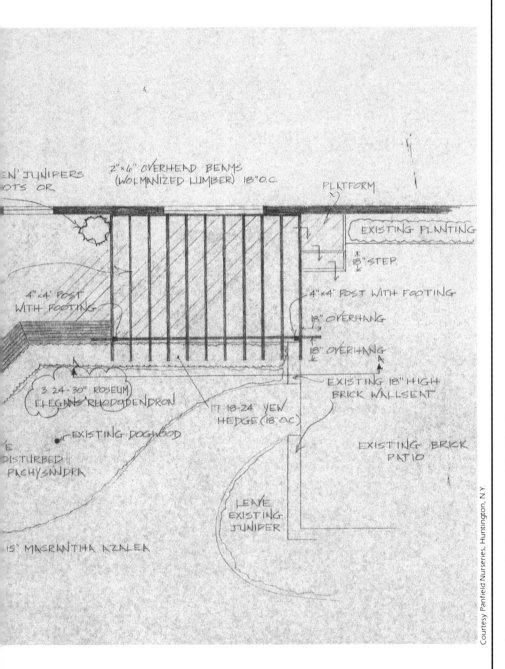

2"×6" OVERHEAD BEAMS
(WOLMANIZED LUMBER) 18"O.C.

EN' JUNIPERS
OTS OR

PLATFORM

EXISTING PLANTING

18" STEP

4"×4" POST
WITH FOOTING

4"×4" POST WITH FOOTING

18" OVERHANG

18" OVERHANG

EXISTING 18" HIGH
BRICK WALLSEAT

3 24-30" ROSEUM
ELEGANS RHODODENDRON

17 18-24" YEW
HEDGE (18" OC)

EXISTING DOGWOOD

EXISTING BRICK
PATIO

DISTURBED
PACHYSANDRA

LEAVE
EXISTING
JUNIPER

15' MACRANTHA AZALEA

Courtesy Panfield Nurseries, Huntington, N.Y.

Creating the Landscape Master Plan

Careful planning is the key to building any open-air design or successfully completing a major landscape project. Besides creating a design that satisfies your personal style, you must choose the building materials needed to create the design and the plant materials needed to make it beautiful. And you must make arrangements for their timely delivery to the project site. If you have the money or don't enjoy working outdoors, you can have all of this taken care of by a professional landscape contractor.

Many people, however, enjoy gardening and yard work and look forward to a major yard project every summer, and because the skills needed to build a deck or patio are easily mastered, many people opt to do all or part of an outdoor room addition themselves. For do-it-yourselfers with no prior experience in planning a major project, organizational details must be given the same priority as the actual building tasks, because oversights here can lead to costly delays that can discourage even a highly motivated person to the point of abandoning the project.

Landscape architects, who understand the pitfalls of outdoor building better than anyone, usually advise their clients to organize a project according to a master plan. And if you retain a landscape architect to help you with the design phase of your project,

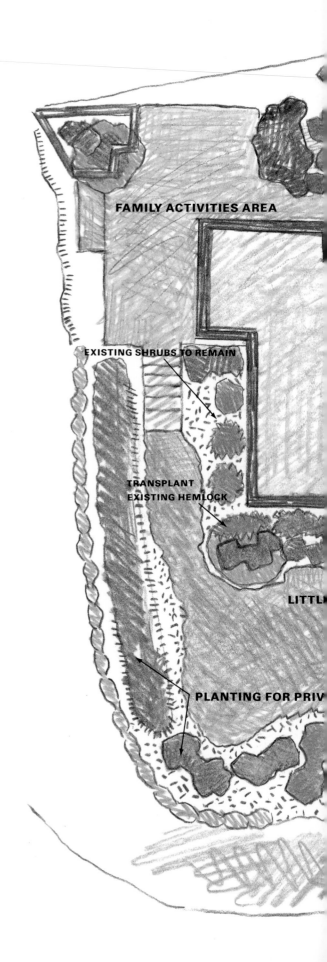

FAMILY ACTIVITIES AREA

EXISTING SHRUBS TO REMAIN

TRANSPLANT EXISTING HEMLOCK

LITTL

PLANTING FOR PRIV

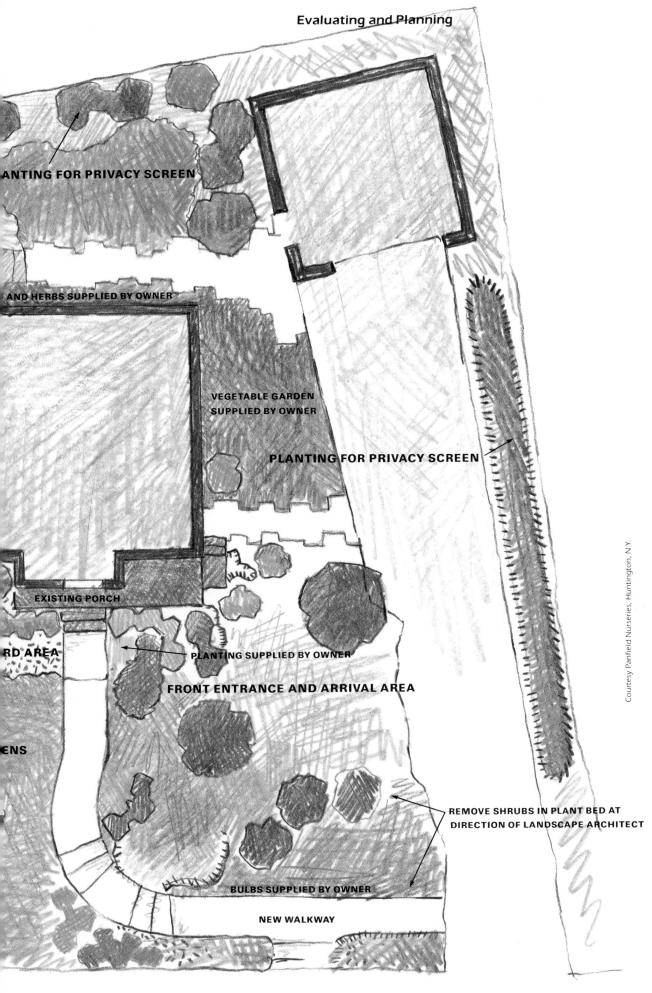

ANTING FOR PRIVACY SCREEN

AND HERBS SUPPLIED BY OWNER

VEGETABLE GARDEN
SUPPLIED BY OWNER

PLANTING FOR PRIVACY SCREEN

EXISTING PORCH

RD AREA

PLANTING SUPPLIED BY OWNER

FRONT ENTRANCE AND ARRIVAL AREA

ENS

REMOVE SHRUBS IN PLANT BED AT
DIRECTION OF LANDSCAPE ARCHITECT

BULBS SUPPLIED BY OWNER

NEW WALKWAY

Courtesy Panfield Nurseries, Huntington, N.Y.

Site-sensitive design is a vital component of outdoor building. Sometimes this means choosing a plan that emphasizes landscape over structure. Here, a simple wood deck becomes a viewing platform for enjoying the surrounding gardens. A more elaborate structure would have destroyed the harmony between nature and the man-made deck.

he or she will provide this service and make sure it includes all aspects of the project. Some nurseries, especially those that have staff designers to assist customers, can also draw up master plans. Hands-on planning aids, such as those marketed by Pro-Creations, can also be used to create a master plan, and, no doubt, there will eventually be computer programs that do the same thing. But any design aid is just that—a mechanical helper that makes it easier for you to express your own ideas about how you want your landscape or outdoor room to look. They do not create the ideas for you and are not a substitute for professional help.

A master plan serves the same purpose in landscaping as a working drawing does for a remodeling project. It shows the work to be done and specifies both the structural and plant materials to be used. It can also point out, and provide remedies for, any potential drainage problems that

you might have discovered when you determined the grade changes. Besides providing a road map, as it were, covering the project from start to finish, it can help you establish priorities. If you don't have enough money to do everything, the plan can break the project into manageable chunks that can be done and paid for over several summers. Approaching a project a section at a time keeps construction schedules and details from overwhelming you.

If you've done no prior landscaping to your property, the professionals recommend that you start by tackling the area around the front entrance, because this is the part of the yard people see first. Most people, however, elect to build a backyard deck or patio as their first outdoor project, because this results in out-door space that can be enjoyed immediately. With your outdoor space complete, you can move on to add a screen of fast-growing shrubs or trees to eliminate unwanted views of your neighbor's yard and to create pleasant ones for yourself. The last priority for a landscape master plan is to spruce up areas of your yard that are little used or seldom seen.

However you establish your own priorities, the master plan should be coded so that each phase is clearly noted, including the tasks to be accomplished and the materials needed to do each job. Many landscape architects use colors to define the various components of the total job, which makes reading the master plan that much easier. And when the project is finally complete, the plan makes a nice piece of art to hang in your study.

Stylish lawn ornaments have a place in open air design, as these oriental guard dogs demonstrate.

Saxon Holt

CHAPTER 3

Special Considerations

I n most cities and towns, any new construction or structural remodeling must be done under the supervision of the local building department. This means taking out a building permit and making sure the design and construction conform to all applicable codes. Unfortunately, too many people, especially those who plan on doing all the work themselves, avoid the building department. Some think their im-

provements will increase their property taxes; others wrongly believe that codes exist solely to ensure that specialized carpentry, plumbing, and electrical work will always be done by licensed professionals, who often charge outrageous prices.

The real purpose of building codes is safety, and to establish a uniform standard of building quality. And it's for this reason that you should always comply with applicable codes and try to overlook that, in a few instances, codes have outlived their usefulness because new technology makes them redundant. Implicit in code compliance are the on-site inspections made by the building department. What must be inspected will depend on the nature of your project and will differ from one locale to another. It is your responsibility to arrange for all required inspections. If you don't, the building department has the authority to order you to tear down everything you have built. And another word of caution: The fine print in many home-insurance policies states that alterations or additions done without a permit or completed without proper inspections can void your coverage. The gamble isn't worth it.

Nancy Hill

Left: **Guardrails are an important safety feature on any deck more than 18 inches above grade, and vitally important on decks off of second story rooms. Skillful designers can incorporate decorative elements that complement the design.**

A visit to your local building department should be an early item on your agenda if you're seriously thinking about any outdoor building. They can tell you if a permit is required for the work and, if so, the procedures you must follow to get one. Permits are usually mandatory for decks, gazebos, and other structural buildings, though unnecessary for patio projects or yard improvements that are more clearly landscaping in nature.

What The Codes Require

Codes that apply to decks are primarily concerned with ensuring proper structural support, or "loading." Many kinds of loadings affect decks; the most important is live loading, which refers to the amount of weight that a deck can hold without collapsing. Live loads include everything that might conceivably be set on the deck temporarily—like people—but does not include the weight of the building materials used in construction. Most codes specify that a deck must be able to support 60 pounds per square foot, though in some areas this is 100 pounds per square foot. If you are building a deck that's stressed (another word used when talking about structural support) to handle a code-mandated live load, it is always better to be safe than sorry. If you know that you'll be using your deck to entertain, it's a good idea to beef up the deck supports to handle up to 100 pounds per square foot, even if the lower figure is acceptable.

If you live in parts of the country that routinely get heavy winter snows, you may also have to comply with code requirements for snow loading—the ability of the deck to support a constant heavy load for a long period of time. And if you're planning on adding a trellis to your deck or are building a freestanding gazebo, the codes will have something to say about correct bracing against the effects of wind. Obviously, the more complex your project, the more codes apply—all the more reason you should have an accurate set of master plans showing what you intend to do. It will help the building inspector advise you about which codes apply.

A skillful designer can create decks that seem to float above the environment, but underneath the beauty there must always be a well-engineered structural system.

Robert Perron

Nancy Hill

Facing page: Structural posts should be mounted on concrete piers that protrude above grade and slope away from the post. Even though treated wood resists moisture-induced rot, posts exposed to puddling conditions will have a shorter life span.

Some Structural Considerations

All buildings start at the ground and work up. With a house, the first step is the foundation; with decks it's the footings. Footings are concrete piers set deep into the ground on which the deck posts rest. Proper footings are important because they carry the weight of the entire deck. Footing holes can be dug either by hand or with a power augering tool, which you can rent. Whichever method you use, it's important to dig the holes to the proper depth so the base of the footing is below the frost line for your part of the country. Footings of insufficient depth will expand and contract as the ground around them freezes and thaws. This can cause the concrete to crack or heave out of the ground, and possibly result in a collapse of the deck. Your building department can tell you how deep to dig (usually between two and five feet). Then the footing holes must be inspected before you pour the concrete to ensure that they are the proper depth.

Footing location is determined by the overall deck dimensions, because the footings support beams that in turn carry the deck joists. Distances between beams depend on what size lumber you select for the joists.

Right: Even properly sloped concrete piers absorb and retain some water which will be absorbed by the posts and lead to rotting. Post caps prevent this by raising the post slightly above the pier. Made of galvanized metal, post caps are impervious to the elements. To secure the post to the cap, drive home 16d (penny) galvanized nails using the pre-drilled holes on the sides of the cap as guides.

Nancy Hill

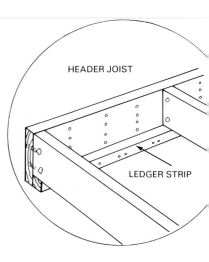

HEADER JOIST

LEDGER STRIP

Below: Support post locations are determined by the distance the beams span and the strength of the wood used to fabricate the beams. For example, the span distance for a doubled 2x12 beam is greater than for a doubled 2x10, so the distance between the posts can be greater; thus, fewer posts need to be used.

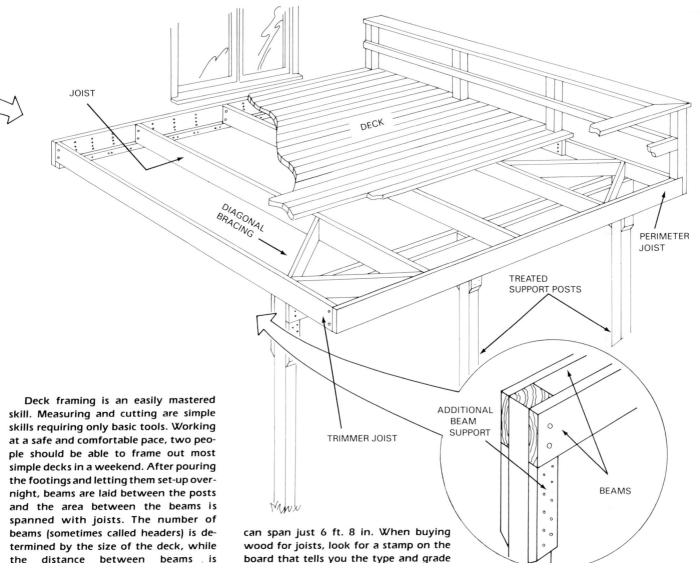

JOIST

DECK

DIAGONAL BRACING

PERIMETER JOIST

TREATED SUPPORT POSTS

ADDITIONAL BEAM SUPPORT

BEAMS

TRIMMER JOIST

Courtesy Wolman Company

Deck framing is an easily mastered skill. Measuring and cutting are simple skills requiring only basic tools. Working at a safe and comfortable pace, two people should be able to frame out most simple decks in a weekend. After pouring the footings and letting them set-up overnight, beams are laid between the posts and the area between the beams is spanned with joists. The number of beams (sometimes called headers) is determined by the size of the deck, while the distance between beams is based on the size of the beam and the amount of structural loading required by local building codes. For large decks, beams will probably be doubled or tripled 2x12s, while for small decks, a doubled 2x8 might be sufficient. Beams should be nailed together from both sides. If a beam must be spliced to achieve the required length, plan the position of the splice so it rests on a post. Joists are single wood members, usually 2x6s or 2x8s. The greater the span, the larger the required joist. Joist separation, called On-Center by carpenters and abbreviated O.C. is also a function of the span. Placing the joists 24 inches O.C. is common for most decks, though beyond certain spans, 16-in. O.C. will be required to avoid sponginess. The type of wood also effects span distances. For example, at 24-inch O.C., a 2x6 joist made of Douglas fir can span 8 ft. 4 in. However 2x6 eastern hemlock joists can span on 7 ft. 8 in. And 2x6 northern white cedar

can span just 6 ft. 8 in. When buying wood for joists, look for a stamp on the board that tells you the type and grade of wood.

The easiest way to install joists is to use joist hangers (see below) using the special short nails sold with the hangers. Alternatively, you can attach a ledger strip of material to a beam (as shown in this illustration). The joist rests on the ledger which gives it added support and keeps it in position for accurate nailing. All deck construction should be done using 16p galvanized nails. The galvanized treatment keeps the nails from rusting and staining the wood. If you opt to use drywall screws for some of the carpentry (only on those parts of the deck that are non-structural) make sure to buy the galvanized variety.

Diagonal bracing at the corners is a good idea especially if the end joist, called either a perimeter or rim joist, is not a doubled member. And when beams do not rest directly on a post, make a support ledger from scrap material to help carry the weight.

Below: When using joist hangers, nail them all to the beam before putting it in place. A good trick is to nail only one side of the hanger. When fitting the joists, the side that was not nailed can be pulled open to more easily accept the joist.

Nancy Hill

A STEP-BY-STEP GUIDE

Footings

1 The first step in building a deck is to lay out the deck's dimensions by stretching line between batterboards—pieces of board nailed horizontally between two stakes. Locate the batterboards beyond the finished deck dimensions so they won't be disturbed during excavation. To check for square, measure the diagonals with a tape. Adjust the staked lines until the two diagonal measurements are equal.

3 Using a power post-hole auger makes digging the holes faster. The tool requires two people and can be rented from most well-equipped tool-rental outlets. Always use caution when working with an auger. Striking a rock can jerk the auger from your hands and create a dangerous situation. Also don't attempt to auger the entire hole at once. Drilling in a series of short lifts keeps the auger from getting stuck in the hole.

2 To locate the center for a post hole, drop a plumb line from the point where the layout intersects.

4 Construction tubes make ideal forms for pouring footings. Available in 10-ft lengths with varying diameters, they can be cut to the correct length with a hand saw. When positioning the tube in the hole, it's important that the top is level.

5 Pour the concrete in lifts—a little at a time. Tamping with a board compacts the concrete and removes voids that diminish its strength. But don't over tamp, or you'll force the aggregate in the concrete to the bottom.

6 After the concrete begins to congeal, use the plumb line to find the center point and insert an anchor bolt to secure the post cap to the footing after the footing completely dries. The L-shaped anchor bolts must be jiggled around to make sure they are completely surrounded by concrete.

7 Using a level and a tape measure, align the post cap so it centers on the center line of the beam or header. When correctly done, the line should bisect the beam or header lengthwise.

Nancy Hill

Below: When designing an overhead structure for a deck or patio, post and beam construction allows for the greatest possible span distance and the fewest number of supporting stuctural members.

Robert Perron

Above and Right: Deck accessories—posts, rail caps, and spindles—milled from pressure treated wood, such as these Life Wood products from Weyerhauser, give homeowners an opportunity to make repairs without undertaking any major rebuilding. They also make it easy to replace a plain railing with a more decorative one.

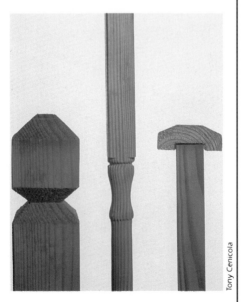

Materials

The basic materials you'll need to build a deck, gazebo, or retaining wall, lay a patio or walkway, or just spruce up the backyard are commonly available at lumberyards and well-stocked home-center stores. For certain types of brick, paving materials, and stone, however, you'll have to shop at a mason's supply yard.

Wood

Wood is the most versatile building material available. Cut it, shape it, bend it, or glue it to create an infinite variety of forms for structural support or pure decoration. Because it can be worked on with basic and readily accessible tools, wood is an ideal material for the homeowner who doesn't have a lot of building experience. And while constructing a deck may seem more complex than a masonry project, cutting and assembling wood is considerably easier than doing the same thing with brick and stone.

For interior building, the most commonly used lumber is No. 2 Douglas fir. Fir and other basic construction-grade lumber, however, will eventually rot if left in direct contact with soil. For this reason, decks and other outdoor structures must be constructed using rot-resistant wood. There are three types to choose from: redwood, cedar, and a manufactured hybrid known as pressure-treated lumber. Less expensive than redwood or cedar, treated lumber is made by injecting preservative chemicals, usually a mixture of copper and arsenic, into medium-grade southern pine. The high-pressure chemical injection gives the wood its characteristic greenish color. Over time, the green hue disappears as the excess chemicals leach out of the wood's pores, and the wood turns a pleasant weathered gray. Like other woods, treated lumber

Right: Different colored stains make it easy to create decorative effects from otherwise ordinary deck boards.

Left: For proper water drainage, deck boards should be installed with an ⅛-inch gap between each board. This gap also allows for expansion. A 16 penny nail, inserted between the boards when nailing them in place, is an excellent spacer for this task.

A small overhead trellis or canopy gives a deck the feeling of having more than one room. When planning any overhead structure, consult a structural engineer to make sure that what you build is correctly braced to withstand wind.

Courtesy Osmose Wood Products

Six-by-eight-inch treated landscape timbers create a retaining wall separating the deck from the upward-sloping yard.

can be painted or stained according to your taste, though for best results you should wait until it's been exposed to the weather for several months and the grayish color begins to appear.

Because of the chemicals that are part of the wood, treated lumber must be handled more carefully than other woods. You should wear gloves when sawing it, and if you must make saw cuts indoors, wear a breathing mask. Scraps of treated wood must be disposed of at a dump and never burned, because burning releases the chemicals. You can imagine the potential danger of arsenic fumes. After working with treated wood, wash your hands thoroughly to ensure they are free from all sawdust and sap.

If all of this sounds as ominous as the printed warning on cigarette packages, that's because the Environmental Protection Agency in 1985 banned the sale to consumers of those toxic chemicals used to preserve wood. It further restricted the type of chemicals that could be used by mills in manufacturing treated wood products and required that treated wood products be tagged with a notification of the chemicals they contain. Despite these precautions, pressure-treated lumber is still the best building material you can buy for outdoor construction, and with careful handling you won't have any problems using it.

If you like the look of redwood or cedar, be prepared to

go deep into your wallet, because the cost difference between treated lumber and the naturally rot-resistant woods is substantial. An alternative is to build the deck's out-of-sight supporting structural components—the joists, braces, and ledger strips—out of treated lumber and use redwood or cedar for the decking boards and trim.

Another popular outdoor wood product is the creosote-treated railroad tie. It's still sold at lumberyards and garden centers, and if you're lucky, you can still find a few laying around, free for the taking, at a railroad yard. Six-by-eight inch and larger ties are ideal for building retaining walls or multi-level pathways. However, recent agricultural research has discovered that creosote may be harmful to plants, so they should not be used in conjunction with planting beds.

When concrete is used for a patio, follow the procedures for pouring a slab on grade: Make sure the soil is well compacted and put down a sand or gravel setting bed. Reinforce the slab with 6x6-inch, 10 gauge, welded, steel mesh and provide control joints for expansion.

Vern Green

Concrete

Concrete is as indispensable as wood. It's required for footings, to set fence posts, and to make retaining walls and sidewalks. When you think about it, it's hard to imagine any outdoor building project that doesn't use this material.

Concrete is actually a mixture of Portland cement, sand, and small stones to which water is added for use. Viscous at first, concrete can be poured into wooden forms to create any shape you want, and when it dries it's almost impervious to damage. Lumber-

Decorative redwood space strips between sections of concrete provide an
aesthetic break from the hard-looking
surface. The spacers also act as control
joints for cracking. When pouring the
concrete they provide a surface for level
screeding—smoothing out the freshly
poured concrete.

Saxon Holt

Herringbone

Basket Weave

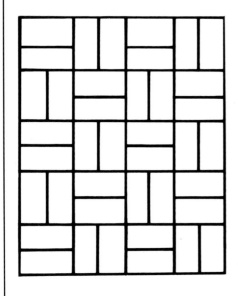

Running Bond

Brick patterns for walks and patios can be as varied as the imagination allows. However, three patterns predominate because they require the fewest number of half bricks. They are Herringbone, Basket Weave, and Running Bond.

yards and home-center stores sell concrete in eighty-pound bags, with each bag yielding three-fifths of a cubic yard. Two "mixes" are commonly available: sand and gravel. Use a sand mix for retaining walls and fence posts. But for footings and anywhere else where the structural support depends on the concrete, use the gravel mix; when set it has greater strength. Another tip: The less water you mix into the concrete the stronger it will be.

Concrete can be mixed in a large wheelbarrow or you can rent a motorized mixer. An alternative is to buy ready-mix concrete and have it delivered to your site from a pumper truck. Concrete bought this way is sold by the cubic yard and there is a minimum order, usually five cubic yards. Some ready-mix companies will be nice and deliver less than a minimum load, though they may charge a stiff service charge for doing it. If you buy concrete this way, make sure you have everything ready when the truck arrives. Pumper drivers work on a tight schedule, and if the "pour" takes longer than they feel was necessary you might be charged an additional fee.

Brick

If your outdoor room centers around a patio instead of a deck, or your plan calls for some new walkways, you'll probably be using brick or some other paving material. If you opt for bricks, remember that for outdoor use they should be dense. Porous bricks are prone to moisture absorption. During winter, this trapped moisture freezes, causing the bricks to crack or flake.

Bricks are sold by the square foot, and individual brick sizes are such that when combined with a half-inch mortar joint they create an even dimension. For example, a three-and-a-half-inch by seven-and-a-half-inch brick is really a four-by-eight when you count the mortar joint. But mortaring bricks is not the best way to lay exterior patios or paths. For better results—and, for that matter, less work in putting them down—consider dry-laying the bricks. In this method, the bricks are set into a bed of mason's sand that has been tamped to provide a firm level under the surface. The advantage of dry-laid bricks becomes evident in the spring. Alternating periods of freezing and thawing during the cold months can cause bricks to lift out of position, or "frost heave," as it's known in the colder parts of the country. When spring comes, the heaved bricks resettle, but seldom back to their original position. If bricks have been set in mortar, you have a major chore on your hands; dry-laid bricks, on the other hand, can be easily removed and reset without disturbing those that haven't been affected by the frost.

No matter which bricklaying method you choose, you'll need to buy a sufficient quantity of mason's sand to make your setting bed. This fine sand is sold by the ton, usually only at a mason's supply yard. As a rule of thumb, one ton equals roughly a cubic yard. Use simple math to determine how much sand you'll need. For example, let's say you're setting pavers on a ten-by-fifteen-foot patio. That's 150 square feet or 21,600 square inches. You want a two-inch-deep setting bed, so multiplying 21,600 by two gives you 43,200 cubic inches. There are 46,656 cubic inches in a cubic yard, so you know that you'll need a little less than a ton of sand to do the job. And something more to remember: When you're buying sand, shop when the weather is nice. Sand absorbs water, which weighs a lot, so sand bought after a rain will yield far less than the normal cubic yard per ton.

Fountains are an attractive outdoor accessory and can be combined with underwater, low-voltage lighting. Any outdoor fountain should be drained for winter if local temperatures go below freezing.

Saxon Holt

A STEP-BY-STEP GUIDE

Bricklaying

3 Place a trial brick at a point where it butts the undisturbed grade. Measure the height of the brick; if it's higher than grade, remove some sand.

1 Make some stakes out of scrap wood and pound them into the ground along the perimeter of the work area. Use longer pieces of scrap wood (batter boards) to bridge the stakes. Adjust the stake height until the boards are level. An alternative to batter boards is to run string between the stakes and level the string with a line level.

4 Start by laying bricks in a corner. After a few are in place, check to make sure they are square by using a carpenter's square.

2 Pour a setting bed of sand into the area between the batter boards; spread the sand evenly using a piece of scrap 2x4 as a screed. When batter boards are used, as they are here, pulling the screed across them automatically levels the sand.

5 To set the bricks firmly into the sand, use a rubber headed mallet and tap lightly. With a properly leveled setting bed, the bricks should be close to level when tapped into place.

6 Make frequent checks to see if the bricks are level using a two- or four-foot carpenter's level. Areas that are not level should be tapped with the rubber mallet until they are level.

7A In a dry-laid installation, sand has the same function as mortar. Shovel a liberal amount of sand onto the bricks and

7B then use a broom to work the sand into the cracks.

8 Add black dirt to the perimeter of the patio to create a smooth transition from the brick to the undisturbed grade.

John Driemen

Keeping Things Safe and Sensible

You've probably already guessed that your new outdoor space will cost you a hefty additional sum in taxes. No sense adding to the misery by doing something foolish that could affect your insurance—or get you sued.

Here are some commonsense tips for working safely with building materials and power tools, keeping a safe work site, and protecting yourself from potential lawsuits.

Using Tools Safely

Good safety habits result naturally when common sense is blended with neatness and an awareness of the other workers around you. Here are some tips to help you make sure that your construction site is a safe one.

• Read the operating instructions before using any power tool.

• Never alter any power tool, for example: removing a blade guard from a power saw.

• Unplug power tools before making any adjustments or changing blades.

• Never use a power tool outdoors when it's raining.

• Keep power tools away from children.

• Keep all debris well away from the work area.

• Wear safety glasses when using any power tools or when cutting, drilling, or shaping masonry.

• Cover any excavations done in the yard.

• If you have an outdoor outlet that is protected with a Ground Fault Interrupter (GFI), use it as your main power source.

• Power cords should be as short as possible and placed in such a way that they are not hazards.

• Never use any power tool in a way not recommended by the manufacturer.

Right: Ground Fault Interrupters (GFIs) must be used for all electrical circuits that have outdoor receptacles. GFIs must be mounted using weather-resistant coverplates that can be closed to seal out moisture. For more information about GFIs turn to page 93.

80

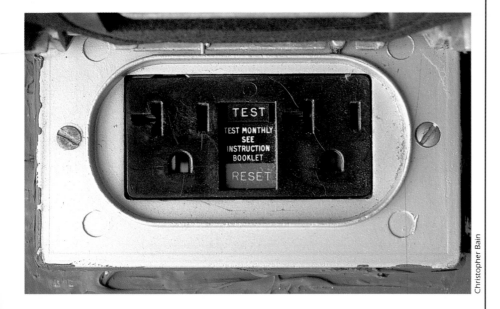

Christopher Bain

Some Plain Common Sense

• Before starting any project, check with your insurance agent to see whether your homeowner's policy covers you for liability claims while the work is in progress. You may have to buy a supplemental policy.

• If you're contracting for all of the work, ask to see a certificate of insurance from your general contractor and from each of the subcontractors. Don't employ any workman who cannot furnish a certificate.

• Some people think that neighborhood kids are a good source of cheap labor. Wrong. Employing a minor without parental consent is a quick ticket to a lawsuit in the event of an accident. And you won't have a leg to stand on.

• Under the law, a construction site is known as an irresistible curiosity. Children are not expected to stay away on their own: it's your responsibility to keep them away. Warn the parents of neighborhood children about what you're doing and post "Keep out" and "No Trespassing" signs around the site. This won't entirely protect you should a youngster wander in and get hurt, but it's strong evidence of your safe intent.

Rules For a Safe Site

• Keep curious children, including your own, away at all times.

• If you've dug footing holes or made any other excavations in your yard, cover the holes with plywood and make an attempt to cordon off the excavated area.

• Make sure all construction debris is promptly put into a dumpster or other refuse container, and arrange for its timely removal.

• Remove all nails from any old or new boards.

• If your yard is fenced, keep the gates locked.

• Keep building materials neatly stacked and out of sight under a tarp.

• Pay attention to overhead power lines when using a ladder or when maneuvering long boards.

• Clean up after each day's work so there is nothing left on the site to trip over or play with.

Christopher Bain

The Basic Tool Kit for Outdoor Building

Nothing is more frustrating than trying to build something using tools that are meant for something else. It can make you so angry that you start thinking seriously about abandoning the project. To keep this ugly situation from developing, here is a list of the tools you should have before you start any deck-building project. Many of the same tools will be needed to build the other projects outlined in this book.

Basic Hand Tools

20-ounce framing hammer

Carpenter's combination square

4-foot level

2-foot level

Plumb bob and line

Crosscut handsaw

7¼-inch power circle saw with a combination blade

¼, ½, and ¾-inch wood chisels

A socket set

Chalk line

A screwdriver set including both slotted and Phillips

25-foot steel tape measure

Power drill with assorted bits

Utility knife

Carpenter's pencils

A tool pouch or nailing apron

For special projects you might have to rent one or more of the following power tools:

A hammer drill, necessary for drilling into masonry wall.

A power mitre saw, a handy tool if you have to cut a large number of boards with angled ends.

An electric cement mixer to mix large quantities of concrete, which saves time if you have a lot of footings to pour.

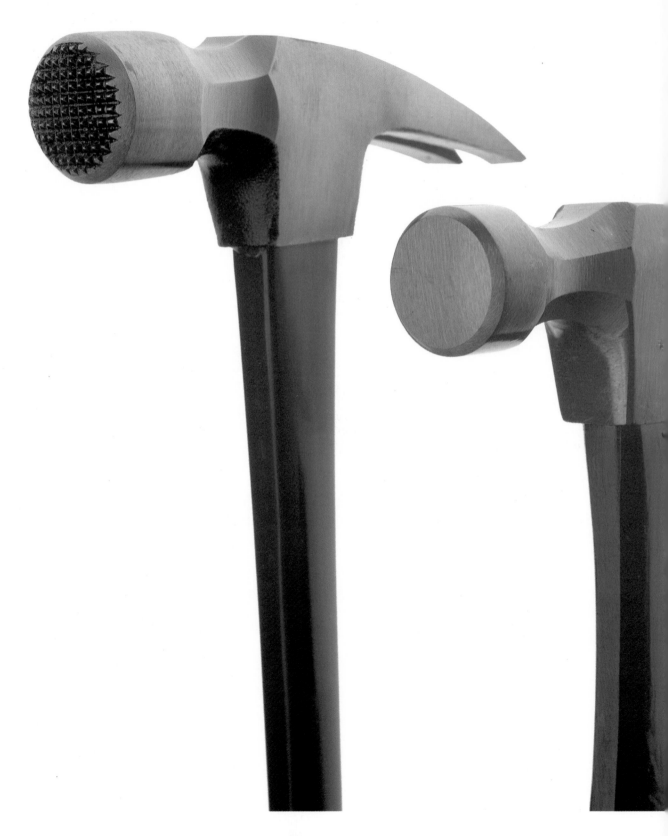

A Tale of Two Hammers

Two hammers are regularly used for building, each intended for specific tasks. The framing hammer (left), with its longer handle and larger striking head, is used for rough carpentry, such as joining large pieces of lumber with big nails. Weighing between sixteen and twenty-two ounces, it's balanced to give the user maximum leverage with less effort. The framing hammer's claw is also inclined at a shallow angle to facilitate removing nails.

The finish hammer (right) is designed for installing trim and moulding and for other light carpentry. It has a smaller hitting area and a shorter handle, giving it the balance needed for the accurate driving of smaller finish nails. The sharply bent claw can remove small nails with minimum damage to the wood.

Most people probably already have this type of hammer laying around the house and are reluctant to spend the money for another, but this is false economy. Because the finish hammer weighs no more than sixteen ounces, trying to drive 16d framing nails with it would quickly become exhausting. In fact, inexpensive finish hammers may break when used for the heavy-duty nailing required in deck building.

When buying a hammer, try it out in the same way you would a golf club. Different brands have different balance points, and you should select one that feels comfortable in your hand. Hammer handles are made from wood, fiberglass, and metal. While wood may eventually break, it provides greater cushioning against the shock of pounding than either the fiberglass or metal handles.

Tony Cenicola

Derek Fell

CHAPTER 4

Outdoor Amenities

In many ways, a deck or patio is like any newly completed addition—empty space waiting to be finished off with personal touches that are the essential ingredients in transforming space into personal comfort.

Because the number one purpose for building an outdoor space is to create an *alfresco* environment for casual entertaining, the first accessory most people want to add is a good barbecue or grill. The different kinds of outdoor grills available today would fill a catalogue thicker than this book. Prices range from under $100 to well over $1,000—and that's for portable models. If you want something more permanent, such as a counter-height brick hearth, be prepared to spend a lot more.

But whatever option you select, there are a few safety rules you should know about and plan for when you're first considering your open-air de-

Facing page: A permanent outdoor barbecue is likely to resemble the masonry work on a house chimney and will carry a similar price tag. Follow the same code requirements as apply to house chimneys and make sure the top extends at least two feet above the highest flammable point.

Right: For many, the covered, propane-fueled barbecue has become a symbol of outdoor life. These barbecues, with the large cooking capacity, are ideal for outdoor parties. Their portability lets them be moved to the most convenient location and stored for the winter.

Christopher Bain

Derek Fell

sign. Where you locate your cooking area is a matter of convenience, though you should be thinking about it right from the project's start. As you look at floor plans for your deck, keep in mind not only where you want to do the cooking, but possible locations for seating areas. As a general rule, you should position the grill so that smoke can't enter the house through open windows and doors. Also, try to locate the grill where it won't obstruct traffic flow onto and off of the deck through the principal access.

If you wish to grill on a moveable charcoal brazier, plan to provide a fireproof base for it. Brick and stone are both good choices. Granted, this isn't always possible on raised decks, but on grade-level decks you can easily accommodate a brick cooking area within the structure of the deck or immediately adjacent to it.

For large, permanently installed masonry barbecues, a brick base is a must. You also must avoid using any flammable materials in the immediate area of any grill. If a barbecue's location is near any trees or high shrubs, trim back the branches to reduce the chance of a misdirected ember or spark causing a fire.

An alternative to a counter or hearth-type barbecue is to dig a fire pit within the deck and build a short masonry chimney that culminates in a charcoal pit. Providing that a brick enclosure completely surrounds the fire, this type of barbecue is safe for wood

New low-voltage products such as post lights from Toro, which define the entrance of this gazebo, provide unlimited lighting options. Mounted on top of a PVC pipe, the light can be cut to any height and mounted to most surfaces.

John Driemen

decks. But a word of caution: treat the cooking facilities on your deck with the same respect for safety as you do your kitchen. Make sure there is a clear area nearby for setting down hot pots and pans as they come off the grill, and keep a fire extinguisher handy for emergencies.

Adding Electricity

We take electricity for granted. Few of us can imagine life without electric coffee makers, can openers, mixers, and, of course, lights. While many people think of their deck and patio as a place where they can rough it a little, a few indoor conveniences add a welcome touch of comfort.

Building electric circuits into a deck is simple, provided that a few precautions are taken. The two types of electrical lines used for outdoor applications are normal 110V (volt) lines and low-voltage lines. If you want to extend your 110V household current to an outdoor space, the job is best left to a professional electrician. On the other hand, installing low-voltage lines is an easy do-it-yourself project (the basic steps are illustrated on pages 94 to 95).

A low-voltage system routes your 110V house current through a transformer, where it is reduced to 12V. This allows the current to be transported through smaller, thinner wires that do not have to be buried or run through a protected conduit or raceway. Your telephone operates on a low-voltage system, for example. Low-voltage systems are also intended for outdoor lighting, because the lower voltage ensures safety if a wire is accidentally cut or a grounding problem occurs.

Like other electrical systems, low-voltage lines can be controlled by switches, and lights can be put on dimmers to create different moods. However, low-voltage lines cannot feed electrical outlets, because their power isn't sufficient to operate electrical appliances.

To service appliances, you must run a branch circuit off of one of your existing house circuits, or, if those circuits are already loaded to the maximum, you must install a new 15-amp circuit to serve the outdoor space. As we said before, this work should be left to a professional, but there are a couple things you should know about before you have the work done.

The National Electric Code (NEC) specifies that the feed line—the wire run from the indoor power source to the outdoor point of use—must be underground and that the conducting wires must be protected by a conduit or similar enclosed raceway. Local electrical codes vary when it comes to distributing the power to outlets around the deck. Some allow you to use a shielded cable, known as a Romex. Others require that all lines be strand wire running through conduit.

Courtesy of Intermatic

Courtesy of Intermatic

Above: Stairways always need light, and a low-voltage fixture is a good way to combine safety and decoration.

The NEC further requires that any outdoor circuit be protected by a Ground Fault Interrupter (GFI). This is a safety device that is either included as part of a receptacle outlet or installed at the panel. The GFI detects slight variations in current flow, and in the event that a person touching a GFI-protected outlet or an appliance plugged into it becomes grounded, the device senses the change of current flow and shuts the system down before the person receives an electric shock. GFI outlets must themselves be protected with weather-tight covers that keep water out.

These safety considerations carry a price tag that is often greater than a homeowner wants to spend. It's possible, in fact, for the electrical contract for installation of a single outdoor circuit to cost more than the building materials needed to construct the deck. But when dealing with electricity, keep in mind that ignoring the codes and safety rules can result in electrical shock or fire and may invalidate your homeowner's insurance.

Facing page: Many low-voltage lights for deck or path mounting have removable shades on top and in the middle of the light globe that allow you to increase the light output.

A STEP-BY-STEP GUIDE

Outdoor Lighting

Outdoor lighting not only creates an enjoyable mood for twilight entertaining, it can also make your backyard or open-air space a safer place. Bordering this walkway are small mushroom lights mounted 12 inches above the ground to illuminate the pathway to a gazebo, while two high-mounted post lights clearly mark the entrance. With the wide variety of outdoor lighting available, it's important that you follow the manufacturer's recommendation when selecting the proper lighting for a given location.

1 Mount the transformer, needed to convert 110 volt house current to the 12 volts that power outdoor lights, at least three feet above grade. The transformer should be positioned close to an outdoor receptacle so that no extension cord is needed. If your house doesn't have an outdoor receptacle, you must install one before using low voltage lighting. This installation is best left to an electrician.

2 A steel pipe or rod is a good tool for making the hole into which the light will be placed. Do not insert the light itself into the hole; it's plastic components will not stand up to the stress of pounding.

3 Connect the light to the power source by using the cable supplied with the light. Usually eight to ten lights can be hooked up to a single cable. For long runs, there are splicing connectors that let you join two lengths of cables. For most outdoor lights, it's simply a matter of penetrating the cable with the sharp pins on the light which function as the electrical connectors. Make the connection with the power on. If it illuminates, you have done it correctly and can then secure the cable. In this model, the mounting spike slips over the connecting pins on the lamp head to make a tight fit.

John Driemen

4 With most outdoor lights, such as this Toro, the cable runs through the hollow mounting spike into the ground. When hooking up a series of lights, allow plenty of slack in the cable between lights. This gives you the option of changing the position of the light at a later date, without having to splice cable.

5 A long screwdriver is an ideal tool to gouge the cable trench that runs between light fixtures. Trench depth should be about six to eight inches—a depth sufficient to minimize the chance of the cable becoming exposed in the event of soil run-off following heavy rain.

6 Mount the assembled light so the base of the lamp is about six inches above the grade; secure it by compressing the soil around it—in much the same way you would secure a plant seedling.

John Driemen

Plumbing

A small sink with running water is a wonderful outdoor amenity that isn't difficult to install. If you're considering a sink, think of it in terms of a wet bar rather than as something intended for cleanup. It should be small and probably stainless steel to resist the weather. Don't spend a lot of money on an expensive faucet that might only corrode over time, and consider running a cold-water line only.

The plumbing principles involved in putting in an outdoor sink are the same as for installing a garden faucet— only the line runs farther. Doing the job is certainly within the ability of anyone who has some patience and is willing to spend a few dollars to buy the right tools.

If your plumbing code allows—and those in thirty states do—the best material for an outdoor water line is Polybutylene Pipe, PB for short. This flexible pipe is easy to cut, and it bends around corners, thus eliminating the need for some pipe joints. For assembling the pipe sections, compression fittings tightened down by wrenches are used, so you don't have to worry about making pipe joints with a blowtorch and solder—a process called sweating—or endure the smell of pipe compounds. (Other non-metallic pipes, for example PVC pipe, do have to be joined by compounds.) A PB T-fitting makes an easy transition from ½-copper pipe. Besides its flexibil-

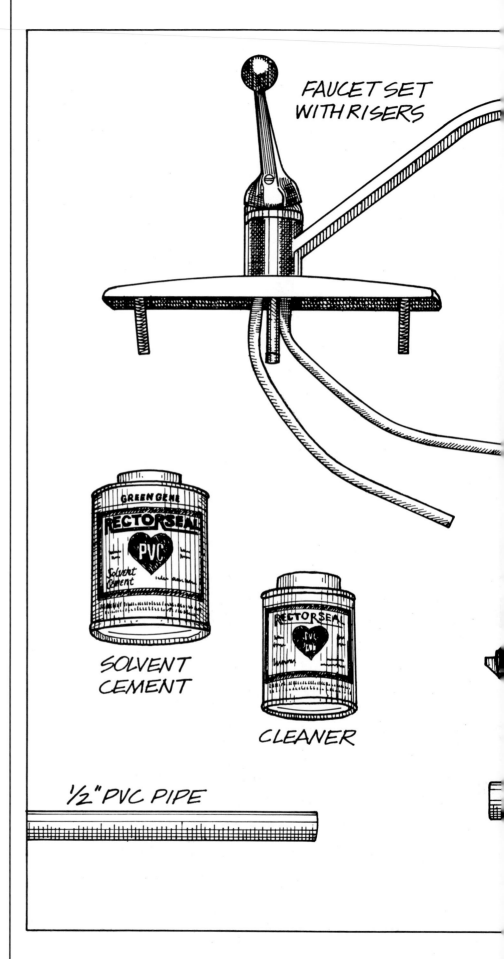

FAUCET SET WITH RISERS

SOLVENT CEMENT

CLEANER

½" PVC PIPE

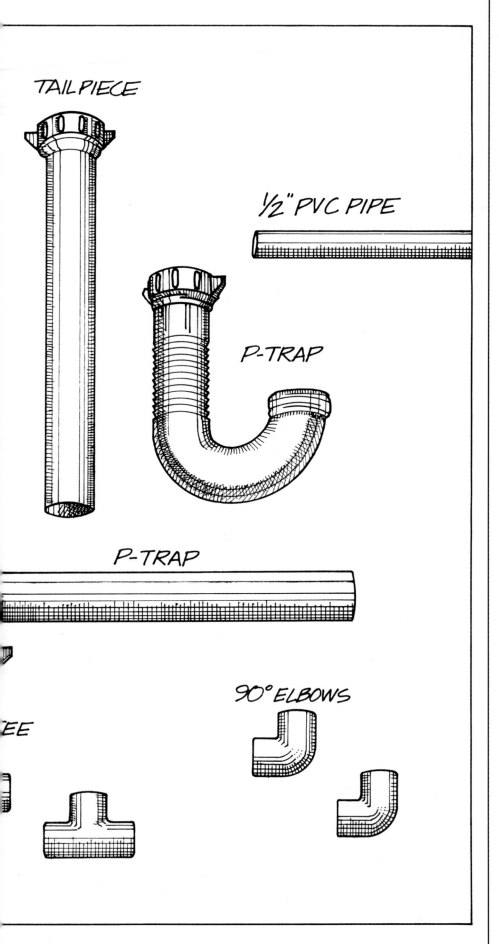

TAILPIECE

½" PVC PIPE

P-TRAP

P-TRAP

TEE

90° ELBOWS

Because modern do-it-yourself PVC plumbing components are easy to work with, you should have no trouble running a simple cold-water line to a wet bar on your deck or patio. Traps, drainpipes, and tailpieces for sinks are 1½ inches in diameter and connect using compression fittings. The water supply line is composed of half-inch PVC pipe, easily cut to length with a handsaw, and whatever half-inch fittings (elbows, couplings, tees) are needed to make them run. To join sections of half-inch PVC, first clean the pipe and fittings with PVC cleaner then apply the PVC pipe cement.

ity, PB will not burst when water freezes inside of it. This added safety feature makes an ideal choice for outdoor use, though you should still always drain the pipes at the end of each season. Whatever plumbing material you choose for an outdoor water line, make sure to include a turn-off valve inside the house as part of the installation.

The drain system for your outdoor sink is even easier to install, because it doesn't connect to your house. All that's needed is to build a French drain—a hole in the ground filled with gravel into which you route the drainpipe. Many people route their gutter downspout into a dry sump to keep puddles from forming after a heavy rain. With a French drain, you don't need to install a trap on the sink, since there are no sewer gasses that must be kept from backing up.

Courtesy of Georgia-Pacific Corporation

CHAPTER 5

Finishing Touches

Now your deck has been built, the last patio paver has been pounded into place, and the new grill is ready and waiting. But the burgers and beer still have to wait a little longer. In the last chapter, we showed you ways to equip your outdoor space with the major amenities. Now it's time to consider the smaller items— the accessories, often taken for granted, but just as important to enjoyable outdoor living.

Furniture and Planters

When it comes to furniture, many people immediately turn to the ubiquitous symbol of backyard life, the round table with it's covering umbrella and the four matching chairs. For something different and probably less expensive, but just as versatile, design and build wooden benches that match the style of your deck. Benches can either be attached to the deck or freestanding, and those permanently installed can be combined with planters. If you've been careful during deck construction, you should have enough wood on hand to build a few benches. The extra material that I recommended you buy to cover waste and mistakes can be used here. And don't throw away any wood scraps longer than two feet. You'll be surprised how useful they can be,

especially for constructing small planters.

A reminder here: benches should be made from the same pressure-treated lumber used to build the deck. So if you have a deck, or you plan to put off building benches and planters for another summer, keep in mind that you can't use standard non-treated construction lumber.

Right: Despite the fact that large, wood planters are heavy, they can still be moved. This allows you to change the feel of any deck.

Left: Built-in deck furniture solves the problems of size and scale on small decks, because it can be built to fit existing conditions. The potential smaller size of built-in furniture means that, when combined with store-bought items, you can accommodate a lot of people without them feeling cramped.

Courtesy of Western Wood Products Association

Courtesy of Western Wood Products Association

Facing page: Chaise lounges are extremely popular for decks and patios. When buying models with removable cushions, plan ahead and have a convenient place to store the cushions and pads during periods of bad weather.

Below: Patio furniture made from steel wire and coated with an outdoor paint is both decorative and functional. Open-wire construction promotes fast drying after rains, and the heavy gauge metal is not likely to be blown around in strong winds.

Saxon Holt

Patio Furniture

If built-in deck furniture is out of the question, or you've had enough building for one summer, you have plenty of inexpensive options when it comes to nice looking tables and chairs. There are as many styles to choose from as there are manufacturers, but whatever you buy, keep in mind these guidelines:

• Deck or patio furniture should be weather-resistant and rustproof. Many tables intended for outdoor use are made with metal that has been painted with an exterior enamel. If the enamel has been baked on, the way it's done on au-

Peter Paige

tomobiles, there should be no rusting problems, provided that the finish doesn't become scratched to the point where the metal is exposed to the weather. Because some scratching is inevitable, you should keep touch-up paint on hand to apply over the worst scratches.

• Aluminum furniture is another popular option. Though it will not rust, aluminum can oxidize, a condition leading to blotches and barnacle-like incrustations on the exposed metal.

• Many small outdoor chairs are made of stiff wire clad in white vinyl. Chairs made this way will, if taken care of, provide years of good ser-

vice. However, you get what you pay for. Inexpensive vinyl-clad chairs skimp on the thickness of the vinyl, and normal wear will expose the metal underneath. Another point to consider is that while white vinyl is resistant to ultraviolet sunlight, the colored vinyls are not and will be damaged by prolonged exposure to sunlight.

• Outdoor furniture should be lightweight so it can be easily moved around to accommodate changing entertainment situations. And it should be collapsible for easy wintertime storage.

• Cushions should be spot resistant, easy to clean, and quick to replace. It

also helps if the small cushions are machine washable.

• Avoid any furniture with glass tops. It may look good, but lots of things can become airborne during a strong wind. Glass tables are extremely vulnerable because their tops are seldom made from tempered glass.

• Because young children are almost the same height as most furniture, you should buy only those items that have rounded corners. Even if you've built a separate play area for your children, the odds are that the adult areas will become their favorite space; rounded corners will greatly reduce the possibility of accidents.

Planters placed near the end of a low deck can call attention to the potential hazard of a drop-off. This is a particularly good safety consideration when the deck is used by senior citizens.

Christopher Bain

Garden Accessories

Plants and flowers are a wonderful way to improve the look of any outdoor space. Even if you have included permanent planters as part of the design, you will probably want to have smaller, moveable planter boxes. Besides offering the possibility of changing your outdoor flower arrangements, moveable planters let you bring the best of your garden indoors when winter comes.

Planter boxes that sit directly on the deck should rest on plates. Otherwise, water seepage will stain the wood and leave an unsightly ring to mark the spot where the box had been. If you're using small clay pots, you might consider buying a small plant stand to keep the pots off the deck. Inexpensive plant stands are sold at garden centers and department stores. If your taste runs to the more ornate

English-style stands, they are available from several mail-order distributors. (Addresses for some of the better mail-order outlets are given on page 115.) Before you do any planting, you should check with a local nursery to find out what kind of potted plants are best for your area. They can also tell you where to place your plants for best results and help choose the right size planter boxes.

Storage

The number of tools and implements you can buy for yard maintenance is staggering—rakes, mowers, edgers, clippers, the list goes on and on. While most people never buy everything that's on the market, what they do buy usually takes up more storage space than is available. As a result, these tools are stored helter-skelter around the house and yard. The garage is a common dumping place for many of them, but they also appear regularly in basements and at inconspicuous locations along the side of the house.

An outdoor remodeling project is an excellent opportunity to create one or more practical storage areas so these seasonal tools can be organized. And the found space you get in other areas of the house and garage will come as a pleasant surprise.

The most common place to keep yard tools is a freestanding shed. Home-center stores sell a variety of different-sized

Christopher Bain

Above: Whiskey barrel planters are ubiquitous at garden centers. They are inexpensive yet large enough for most plants.

Below: Crawl spaces under houses are potential storage bonanzas, but when creating an access to a crawl space make sure to install a child-proof lock.

Christopher Bain

sheds. They are prefabricated for easy assembly and can be placed directly on the ground. For better protection, however, you should consider pouring a cement slab or laying a pad of dry-laid bricks. Because these sheds are not structural in the same sense that a gazebo is, they do not require footings. Backyard sheds are inexpensive and are often used as sales items to entice customers into the store. They are not terribly attractive, however, and because most are constructed from galvanized metal that's been painted, they will need occasional maintenance.

If you are building a raised deck, a good storage area can be found underneath it. Because a raised deck provides some shelter from the elements, it's a good location for keeping tools when other options aren't available. Hanging rakes, hoes, and other long-handled tools from either the back wall or brackets mounted on the support posts is a good way to keep them neat and ready to use. On the deck itself, you might consider an enclosed bench with a lid—a design that resembles a child's toy chest. This is an ideal spot to keep anything from charcoal and starter fluid to spare clay flowerpots.

Sheds are the best way to store and organize outdoor tools, furniture, and garden accessories. If you don't have the space for a large shed like this one or even one of the smaller prefabricated models, consider setting aside part of your garage for storage.

Below: Older homes with porches usually have an area under the porch that's not used. This can be utilized for storing items you don't really care about damaging. If you use this area for wood storage, be careful that it doesn't become a breeding ground for termites.

Facing page: The area under a deck is usually a disaster zone of weeds and debris that has slipped through the cracks between the deck boards. While it's difficult to stop the weeds from growing, the area can be screened using lattice panels.

Jack Schneider/Illustrator's Stock Photos

Christopher Bain

Saxon Holt

Outdoor Food Service

Utensils for outdoor eating or entertaining should be chosen with a strong bias toward common sense. The wind can hurl debris onto a glass table-top and turn plates and glasses into airborne missiles. For this reason, plastic dinnerware may be the best choice for outdoor eating and entertaining. Plastic items are also more durable, and because they cost less than glass and china, you won't be upset if they break.

Plastic utensils are also a must if you have a swimming pool. In this case, broken glass can be a serious safety hazard, because in water it's virtually invisible.

In this example of what not to do, a glass table has been placed directly under a group of trees. As pleasing as it might be, falling branches could easily break or crack the glass. If you want this type of seating, a better choice is to select a table made from a non-breakable material.

Christopher Bain

Sources
and Index

Outdoor living spaces—decks, patios, terraces, etc.—are built from generic materials: wood, nails, brick, stone, and concrete. The best place to get information about these materials is from the dealers in your area who sell them. To track them down use your telephone directory, where you'll find everything you need listed under the categories of Building Supplies, Masonry Supplies, and Hardware.

The sources given below comprise neither a complete nor comprehensive list. Rather, they are starting points that will guide you to information on materials, tools, and topics that can help you with your outdoor projects.

ASSOCIATIONS

National Association of Home Builders (NAHB)
15th and M Streets NW
Washington, DC 20005

American Institute of Architects (AIA)
1735 New York Avenue NW
Washington, DC 20006

Western Wood Products Association
Yeon Building
522 SW Fifth Avenue
Portland, OR 97204

American Home Lighting Institute (AHLI)
435 N. Michigan Avenue
Chicago, IL 60611

Portland Cement Association
5420 Old Orchard Road
Skokie, IL 60076

BUILDING PRODUCTS

Georgia Pacific
Box 48408
Atlanta, GA 30362

Harlan Metal Products
230 West Carob Street
Compton, CA 90220

Kopper Pressure Treated Wood Products
Koppers Co. Inc.
1900 Koppers Building
Pittsburgh, PA 15219

Osmose Wood Products
P.O. Drawer O
Griffin, GA 30224

Simpson Strong-Tie Connectors
1450 Doolittle Drive
Box 1568
San Leandro, CA 94577

TECO
5530 Wisconsin Avenue
Chevy Chase, MD 20815

Weyerhaeuser Life Wood Products
Weyerhaeuser Co.
Tacoma, WA 98477

DECK AND GARDEN FURNITURE

Backhouse Inc.
4121 Hillsboro Road
Suite 301
Nashville, TN 37215

Country Casual
17317 Germantown Road
Germantown, MD 02165

Reed Bros.
Turner Station
Sebastopol, CA 95472

Simms & Thayer
205 Oak Street
Pembroke, MA 02359

The Wickerworks
267 8th Street
San Francisco, CA 94103

GAZEBOS

Jim Dalton Garden House
7260-68 Oakley Street
Philadelphia, PA 19111

Vintage Gazebos
Dept. 367
513 S. Adams
Fredericksburg, TX 78624

Vixin Hill
Dept. GD
RD #2
Phoenixville, PA 19460

LIGHTING

Arroyo Craftsman
127 E. St. Joseph Street
Arcadia, CA 91006

Hanover Lantern
Divison of Hoffman
Products Inc.
470 High Street
Hanover, PA 17331

Loran Inc.
1705 East Colton Avenue
Redlands, CA 92373

TORO
5300 Shoreline Blvd.
Mound, MN 55364

MISCELLANEOUS ACCESSORIES

Clappers Garden Catalog
1125 Washington Street
West Newton, MA 02165

Conrans
160 E. 54th Street
New York, NY 10022

Crate and Barrel
Box 3057
Northbrook, IL 60065

Lillian Vernon Corp.
510 S. Fulton Avenue
Mount Vernon, NY 10550

Lord & Burnham
PO Box 255
Irvington, NY 10533

Smith & Hawken
25 Corte Madera
Mill Valley, CA 94941

Williams-Sonoma
Box 7456
San Francisco, CA 94120

PAINTS AND STAINS

Samuel Cabot Inc.
One Union Street
Boston, MA 02103

The Flood Company
Box 399
Hudson, OH 44236

Lucas Wood Stains
The Lucas Group
Cleveland, OH 44115

Olympic Stain
2233 112th Avenue NE
Belleview, WA 98004

Pittsburgh Paints
PPG Industries
One PPG Place
Pittsburgh, PA 15272

TOOL MANUFACTURERS

Black & Decker
Box 798
Hunt Valley, MD 21030

Disston Tools
The Disston Co.
Danville, VA 24540

Estwing
2647 8th Street
Rockford, IL 61101

Makita Tools
12950 E. Alondra Blvd.
Cerritos, CA 90701

Porter Cable Tools
Box 2468
Jackson, TN 38302

Ryobi Tools
1158 Tower Lane
Bensenville, IL 60106

The Skil Corp.
4801 W. Peterson Avenue
Chicago, IL 60646

Stanley Tools
New Britain, CT 06050

Index

METRIC CONVERSION CHART

UNIT	ABBREVIATION OR SYMBOL	METRIC EQUIVALENT
mile	mi	1.609 kilometers
rod	rd	5.029 meters
yard	yd	0.9144 meters
foot	ft *or* '	30.48 centimeters
inch	in *or* "	2.54 centimeters
square mile	sq mi *or* m^2	2.590 square kilometers
acre	acre	4047 square meters
square rod	sq rd *or* rd^2	25.293 square meters
square yard	sq yd *or* yd^2	0.836 square meter
square foot	sq ft *or* ft^2	0.093 square meter
square inch	sq in *or* in^2	6.452 square centimeters
cubic yard	cu yd *or* yd^3	0.765 cubic meter
cubic foot	cu ft *or* ft^3	0.028 cubic meter
cubic inch	cu in *or* in^3	16.387 cubic centimeters
ton	ton	0.907 metric ton
pound	lb or #	0.454 kilogram
ounce	oz	28.350 grams